Canada
My *"FurEver"* Home

Codi's Adventures

Ages 6 - 10

Copyright © 2018 by Norma Fay Nicholson. 779889

ISBN:	Softcover	978-1-9845-4010-2
	EBook	978-1-9845-4009-6

All rights reserved. No part of this book may be reproduced or transmitted in any form or by any means, electronic or mechanical, including photocopying, recording, or by any information storage and retrieval system, without permission in writing from the copyright owner.

Print information available on the last page

Rev. date: 07/10/2018

To order additional copies of this book, contact:
Xlibris
1-888-795-4274
www.Xlibris.com
Orders@Xlibris.com

Canada
My "*FurEver*" Home

First Year as a Canadian Citizen

Written by

Norma Fay Nicholson

for

Codi Nicholson

For my parents, Noel and Norma;
my sisters, Judith and Kosu;
my foster mom, EK Park;
my trainer, Elena;
my sitters, Vivian, Max, and Joseph;
and my vet, Dr. Akeem.

I am living a happy life in Canada
with your help and loving it!

Your love and caring have kept me happy and healthy.

Contents

The Purpose of Writing My First Book viii
Across the Ocean with a New Name 1
Arrival in Canada 2
Starting Life in My Forever Country My Foster Mom, EK 4
The Road to Freedom 6
Meeting My Adoptive Parents 8
Introduction to My New Environment 10
Bye to My Foster Mom 12
Home At Last 14
Visit to My Canadian Vet 16
Opportunities to Learn 18
I Am a Big Boy Now 20
Read My Second Book Next Year 22

The Purpose of Writing My First Book

To have my adopted parents write the story of my rescue and share with the whole world

To encourage children between the ages of 6 – 10 years to read adventurous stories

To thank everyone who assisted in saving my life and creating the opportunity for me to live in a wonderful country as Canada

To encourage and inspire others to think about adoption by rescuing pets, because we can be companions and we can be great addition to families

To ensure my adopted parents continue to write a series of books updating readers until I am eight years old in human years.

One human year equals seven dog years; I will actually be fifty-four years of age!

Across the Ocean with a New Name

I am no longer known as Cookie (my Korean name). I am now Codi, who is a handsome male poodle covered in thick black fur and with shining grayish-brown eyes and a cute face. I am two and half years old.

I love my new name and always look at you when I hear my beautiful name. I am very happy to tell you about my adventurous life.

My country of birth is far away from Canada. I was born on an animal farm in South Korea. I am very lucky to have been chosen to come to Canada to find a new home. This was a very happy moment for me. Many small dogs like me are taken to the markets in my country and sold as food.

I was rescued by a not-for-profit organization based in Canada. EK and her team come to my country every year and pay the farmers to grow produce for the market in exchange for the selling of pets. They find loving homes for us in Canada.

I traveled for eleven hours by plane to get to Canada. To be safe on the plane, I was placed in a large crate with other rescued pets that were seeking forever homes like me. I do not like being in a crate because this reminds me of the way that small dogs are taken to the market.

Quiz Corner

1. Where is the country of my birth?
2. Do you live in a loving family? What does this mean?
3. How far is South Korea from Toronto?

Arrival in Canada

I arrived in Canada on a plane, which landed at a very large airport by the name of Toronto Pearson IInternational. It was a sunny day, and I was very hot. I barked and cried while waiting. I did not like the new sights, sounds, and many people and vehicles that I saw.

I was very restless and wanted to get out of the crate, but I was kept confined until immigration officers checked us to ensure that we were all healthy.

I saw myself as a precious cargo, and it was great to hear the good news: "You are healthy. Now out the crate. Go with your foster mom."

EK, my *"savior"* and foster mom, took several of us to her beautiful home. It is very emotional to tell you how happy I was to be finally out of a crate, where I felt like I was choking. I do not want to ever go back into one. I felt my body trembling with joy as I departed from the crate.

Quiz Corner

4. Who is a foster mom?
5. Describe a crate.
6. Why do pets need to have healthy meals?

Starting Life in My Forever Country
My Foster Mom, EK

At my foster home, I slept in a big bed for the very first time in my life! I really felt loved. I received healthy food, water, and many hugs. I even got to play with toys and sleep in late!

My foster mom is responsible for ensuring that a loving family adopts me. She screens applications and talks with all potential adopters. EK took my picture and, with information about my life, added this to a webpage on the internet. This allows many people to look at my picture, read my history, and decide if I will be the pet they are looking for.

Potential adoptive parents complete an online application about themselves and what kind of home they are able to provide for a pet. EK reviews all applications and speaks with each potential adopter on the phone. She asks many questions and provides lots of information about my background at this visit. When she is satisfied that she has found a loving family, she arranges a convenient time to take me to visit them.

Quiz Corner

7. Who are foster parents?
8. What is the name of a toy that you would give to pets?
9. Share something that makes you really happy.

The Road to Freedom

At my foster mom's home, there are many pets that are waiting for new homes. My foster mom owns a jeep (which is bigger than a car), so she is able to drive several of us at a time to visit potential adoptive parents.

On the day arranged for my visit to my potential adoptive parents, I was tethered with two other pets to my foster mom's waist and driven in the jeep to meet them.

I had not seen the city before, and I held my head out the window of the jeep so that I could look around as EK drove. I saw large buildings and big streets with many cars and trucks being driven on them. I loved the warm air on my face. I thought, *This is what freedom feels like!*

After what seemed like a very long time, the jeep pulled into a tree-lined street, and I saw some people standing on their porch, waving at us. I could not wait to get outside! EK parked and then took us out of the vehicle. I wagged my tail and jumped up on their porch.

Quiz Corner

10. Do you know what is meant by *freedom*?
11. What prevented me from falling out the window as the jeep wa
12. When a dog wags its tail, what is the dog telling you?

Meeting My Adoptive Parents

Four of my new family members were on the porch to greet me—Noel, Norma, Judy, and Kosu. My loving mom, Norma, scooped me off the floor and gave me great big hugs. I then received hugs and kisses from all other family members. I think they must have seen how happy I was, because they chose me from among the two pets that were welcomed to their home.

They talked with me, and all were very happy to see me. I did not understand any English, but because they were all smiling, I thought to myself, *I think I am adopted. I have a real family.* I was so happy! They took pictures of me and gave one to my foster mom to place on the internet.

Family members asked my foster mom many questions, such as, was I potty trained outside? Did I sleep through the night? How far could I walk without getting tired? What did I like to eat? Could I play with children, and was there anything special about me that they should know in order to take good care of me?

I listened to the discussion and wished I could say, "Take me please. Give me lots of love and a nice home. I need nothing more."

Quiz Corner

13. Who are adoptive parents?
14. Why do you think I was so happy?
15. Do you love getting hugs, and why?

Introduction to My New Environment

My foster mom needed to ensure that I would love being with my adoptive parents. She suggested that my family take me to the backyard to walk around and participate in play with me while she observed.

I was so happy. I ran around the perimeter of the backyard and held my face to the ground. I could not believe that this would be my home. I saw lots of toys, flowers, green grass, and a fenced-in backyard in which I could safely play.

Before my foster mom left, my new family took me for a long walk. They took turns carrying me, as I was not used to wearing a leash and did not know which direction I should go when I was wearing it. On our return, I was given my supper in my own blue bowl. I also received a smaller blue bowl for my water—my own dishes that I did not have to share!

Judy and Kosu returned to their home. Before they left, they gave my parents additional instructions on ways to take care of me, such as ensuring that I was taken for walks during the night.

EK got into her vehicle with the two other pets that were being taken to meet potential adoptive parents. My mom, dad, and waved goodbye, and they thanked her for bringing me into their lives.

My parents are very brave, because they are retired seniors and I am their first pet! I am not yet potty trained outside, so I have accidents at times. I do not understand some commands and house rules. They love caring for me and do not get upset. I try not to have accidents, and they strive to take me outside as often

Quiz Corner

16. Why is it that I was not potty trained outside?
17. What is meant by "having an accident"?
18. Why is it that I did not understand English?

Bye to My Foster Mom

It is very hard to explain how one can be sad and yet happy at the same time. I watched as my foster mom got into her vehicle and as she waved goodbye, and I felt sad that I would not see her again. I also watched as my adoptive parents smiled and waved goodbye, and then my dad scooped me up into his arms and gave me a big hug.

My parents know a lot of our neighbors, and they were informed that *a pet* was coming to live next door, so I was taken to meet both of my parents' neighbours.

They were also very happy to see me and asked if I understood any English. My parents said they would need to help me get adjusted by not only saying words but also showing me the actions that align with the words.

My parents described me as being witty and smart and would therefore learn to understand English in a short time.

Quiz Corner

19. Why did I experience two sets of emotions?
20. What does it mean to have neighbors?
21. In what way are you witty and smart?

Home At Last

It was my bedtime! Oh no! My parents got my bed ready with a warm blanket inside a crate and added a toy. They played and talked with me, then they placed me in the crate, covered it with a pretty sheet, and said good night.

I was very scared! I cried and barked very loudly. I was so nervous that I used my mouth and my feet to pull the covers off the top of the crate and shredded the sheet into small pieces. I was so upset that I slept for short periods only.

My parents came to see me many times during the night, spoke softly to me, and said, "It will soon be morning, and you will be taken out of the crate." I don't think that they slept either. I wished that I could be taken out of the crate. When I did not see my parents, I was so nervous that I had many accidents.

They came to see me very early in the morning and seemed sad that I was unable to sleep all night. I was taken out of the crate and received big hugs and my breakfast.

There were lots of walking and playtime during the days ahead. I loved being free to run and play, and I listened to understand. I became more playful and friendly.

On my second night at home, my parents encouraged me to sleep in my own doggie bed beside them in their bedroom. I was so happy and did not mind being awakened a few times to go potty outside.

Quiz Corner

22. Why was I afraid to sleep in a crate?
23. What did I do to get my parents' attention during the night?
24. Where did I sleep on my second night at home?

Visit to My Canadian Vet

Shortly before leaving South Korea, I was taken to a vet to ensure that I obtained a veterinary certificate of health, which would indicate I was healthy to travel to Canada. My understanding is that I would be turned away and not be able to go on the plane if I did not receive all my vaccinations and be free of infectious or contagious disease and if I did not get the documentation that showed that I posed no danger to public health.

I received a *clean bill* of health, and my parents took a copy of my South Korean certificate of health to my Canadian vet, Dr. Akeem. I was examined in the office and saw other pets waiting for other health services.

I love going to visit my Canadian vet. I receive treats and gentle caring, and I really love it when he says, "Codi, so good to see you."

He helps my parents understand my health and the follow-up care that will be required to maintain optimal health as I grow. He knows that I do not like needles and tries to minimize how much blood work I need or medication that requires an injection.

Quiz Corner

25. What kind of doctor is a vet?
26. Where does this doctor work?
27. Name a reason why you would take your pet to see a vet.

Opportunities to Learn

My parents decided that they needed help in getting me potty trained. I continued to have accidents inside even when they took me outside every two hours during the day.

I really tried not to have accidents and to wait until they were able to take me outside, but this happened several times, especially early in the mornings and at night. I did not know how to indicate to them when I needed to go potty.

Back in South Korea, on the farm, I lived, ate, and slept in a crate. I was only taken out of the crate whenever the decision was being made if it was my turn to go to the market to be sold for food.

My parents found a wonderful trainer by the name of Elena. She even came to our home so that I could be trained in my very own backyard. She loves pets, has one of her own, and provides special training and sleepover for pets. She was very patient with me and spoke lots of times with my parents while directing them on the different ways to support me to be successful.

Remember that my parents introduced me to our neighbors and said that I was *witty and smart*? I had these opportunities to show them how right they had been.

I now go to the back door and scratch the door, which indicates I need to go outside, and I do the same on the other side of the door when I am ready to return indoors. When I go for walks with my parents, I wear my leash and I stop a bathroom." They always bring "scoop" bags to ensure that my poop is the bins that are provided by our city.

Quiz Corner

28. Why did I need a trainer?
29. Do you require training in anything new?
30. State one way in which my success was measured.

I Am a Big Boy Now

I have been living in Canada for one year, and my life has changed so much! Words cannot describe how happy I am. Yet I continue to have some anxieties. I stay with a sitter when my parents are away

Things That Make Me Happy

- Having weekly short stays with my sitters, Viv and Max
- Having the ability to go outdoors even during a winter ice storm (my full-body fur keeps me warm)
- Having passionate and caring parents who demonstrate their love every day
- Meeting new folks and other pets every day and being able to interact with them
- Enjoying long walks in the parks and playing with my toys
- Spending quiet time with my parents when we relax on the coach, snuggle, and watch TV
- Playing with a variety of toys and having three special spaces of my own to relax—a soft mat and two beds
- Having the variety of meals and snacks that my parents prepare for me
- Visiting seniors in their residences
- Chasing squirrels, birds, and wild rabbits

Things That Make Me Unhappy

- I get very anxious and scared when left alone even for ten minutes. I have accidents during those times.
- I love the smell of chocolate and spices, but I cannot eat those foods because I would become ill.

Quiz Corner

31. Why would I need a sitter?
32. What are the names of my sitters?

Read My Second Book Next Year

I will begin my training to become a therapy dog to cheer up seniors in nursing homes.

My parents hope this volunteer role will help me build my confidence and may result in lessening my anxiety.

Do write to my mom and tell her what you liked about my first book and also what you would like to see included in my second book.

authornormanicholson@gmail.com

Answers to Quiz Corner

1. South Korea
2. I feel safe (one example)
3. South Korea is 8,000 miles from Toronto
4. Rescues and prepares for adoptive parents
5. Usually squared shape with different heights and widths, made from wire
6. Stay healthy
7. Provide loving home while waiting for adoption
8. A soft ball
9. Playing with friends (one example)
10. Being free to play
11. Leash on
12. I am happy
13. New loving parents
14. Need a loving family
15. Feels warm and loved
16. Lived, ate and slept in a crate, not allowed outside
17. Go to bathroom on the carpet or floor
18. In my country of birth, most spoke Korean
19. Love foster and adoptive parents
20. People living near to your home
21. Understand many directions and instructions
22. Reminds me of what happened in the past
23. Cried
24. My own bed in my parents' bedroom
25. Make sure pets are healthy
26. Special animal doctor
27. Pet is sick
28. Helps to learn new things
29. To ride a bicycle (example)
30. I have no more accidents
31. Anxious and do not like staying by myself
32. Viv, Max and Joe

CPSIA information can be obtained at www.ICGtesting.com
Printed in the USA
LVIW01n1612210718
584471LV00002B/1